This journal belongs to:

____

Published by Joyful Journals

2019